VIOLIN SOLO • PIANO

HALLELUJAH

FOR VIOLIN AND PIANO

ARRANGED BY

T0039567

www.lindseystirling.com
www.facebook.com/lindseystirlingmusic
twitter.com/LindseyStirling

ISBN 978-1-5400-0692-9

7777 W. BLUEMOUND RD. P.O. BOX 13819 MILWAUKEE, WI 53213

Visit Hal Leonard Online at
www.halleonard.com

HALLELUJAH

Words and Music by LEONARD COHEN
Arranged by Lindsey Stirling
Piano arrangement by David Russell
and Jennifer Stirling

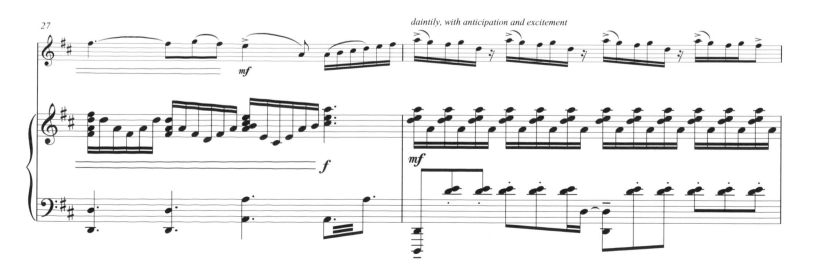

HALLELUJAH

FOR VIOLIN AND PIANO

ARRANGED BY

www.lindseystirling.com
www.facebook.com/lindseystirlingmusic
twitter.com/LindseyStirling

ISBN 978-1-5400-0692-9

7777 W. BLUEMOUND RD. P.O.BOX 13819 MILWAUKEE, WI 53213

Visit Hal Leonard Online at
www.halleonard.com

HL00250149

HALLELUJAH

Words and Music by LEONARD COHEN
Arranged by Lindsey Stirling
Piano arrangement by David Russell
and Jennifer Stirling

daintily, with anticipation and excitement

with resolve

solo, reverently

rall.

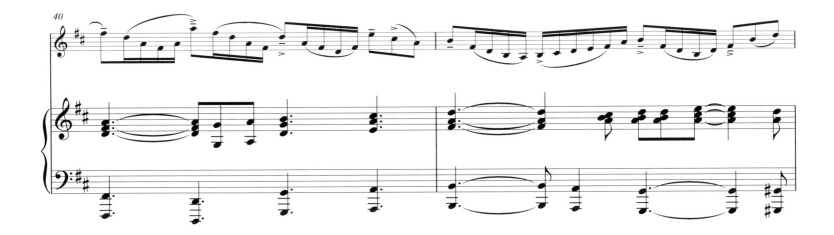

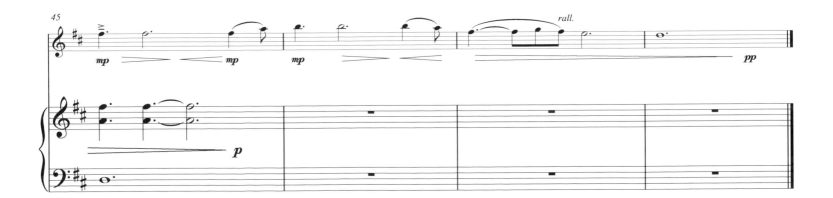

Also available:

PHANTOM OF THE OPERA
Violin Solo/Piano   00109716 $9.99

BEAUTY AND THE BEAST
Violin Solo/Piano   00238143 $9.99

LINDSEY STIRLING FAVORITES
Violin Play-Along   00159634 $19.99

LINDSEY STIRLING HITS
Violin Play-Along   00123128 $19.99